DRIED FLOWER

Love

DRIED FLOWER

Love

*Make 18 Inspiring
Projects for Your Home*

IVANA JOST

SCHIFFER
CRAFT

4880 Lower Valley Road • Atglen, PA 19310

Contents

About This Book

Living in a mountain village as a child, I was always surrounded by nature; it's something that's reflected in my choice of profession as a florist, something that I have always needed around me, and something that I love. Above all, the fresh flowers and plants fascinated me with their beauty and transience, reflecting the cycle of nature throughout the seasons.

But then I discovered dried flowers. I realized that preserving flowers, grasses, and branches does not disturb the natural cycle but rather conserves the beauty of the plants for longer. From something that was predetermined to wither and die, a thing of lasting beauty emerges without losing any of its nature. This realization gave me a fresh perspective on the possibilities presented by dried flowers; I had fallen in love with them.

Thanks to the durability of the materials, arranging dried flowers offers endless variety. In this book, I would like to show you some arrangements, which are small projects close to my heart. You'll find instructions for various techniques and where to use them, as well as encouragement and inspiration to open yourself to the world of dried flowers and make your own creations.

I wish you every success with the projects in this book, creative inspiration, and, above all, lots of joy when working with dried flowers.

The Basics

Dried Flowers – the New Trend

In recent years, dried flowers have experienced a resurgence. But for this old, dusty style of décor to celebrate such a comeback, several factors had to come together.

Awareness of sustainability keeps growing, and it's no longer of interest only to environmental activists. Sustainability is the correct direction for the development of our society. The worlds of politics and business are making their contributions through new ecological regulations. Furthermore, increasing numbers of us have a serious desire to protect the environment and to change something for the better.

This societal change of thinking takes people back to their roots, to nature itself. Consumers are becoming increasingly aware, with more value placed on local and seasonal produce. And the trend is moving away from the throwaway society and toward ecologically responsible trade.

The COVID-19 pandemic further strengthened this movement. People were forced to spend an unusual amount of time in their own four walls; many used this time to redecorate or reconfigure their living space. These renovations placed much more emphasis on cozy and natural materials. Dried flowers are perfectly suited to these trends because they stand for durability and recyclability in a way that practically no other (natural) product does. Something that was once fresh and has long since passed its peak can still fulfill a second, no less important, purpose.

Finding, harvesting, and drying the flowers and grasses before the creative work can even start takes a great deal of time. And if there's no chance of plundering these treasures from your garden or you need to complete a project quickly, a visit to a specialist shop is a good alternative. Thanks to the increasing demand for dried flowers, flower and craft stores carry a good selection of dried botanicals.

The projects presented in this book usually require a certain number of dried flowers. The most-beautiful arrangements are created through the skillful combination of the most-varied materials. If you want to immediately start your homemade projects, buy a selection of dried flowers from your favorite store. The range of dried flowers is constantly growing, and chances are good you'll find exactly what you are looking for.

It's still a very special experience to go in search of plants that are suitable for drying; to experience the diversity and beauty of nature on this journey of discovery; to sense the material, color, shape, and scent when picking them; and to observe the process of change and transience when drying them. It takes time and patience, but you are rewarded with new knowledge and experience in the world of dried flowers. This is a part of the creative process, just as the arranging is itself.

Be it in your own garden, the woods, or in the meadows, nature in her full diversity offers countless plants whose flowers and fruits are suitable for drying. If you observe a few basic rules, they are stunningly beautiful in their dried state and can be kept for a very long time.

Sun

Dried flowers suffer in direct sunlight. Of course, they don't need to be kept in a dark room, but direct sunlight quickly fades their beautiful natural colors. A velvet green eucalyptus will be almost bleached white after a few weeks in full sunlight, and a pink hydrangea turns into a brown head. If you want to enjoy your dried flowers for years to come, then place your arrangement somewhere protected from the sun, or work with very light materials that won't fade too badly.

Moisture

Their name gives us a big clue—dried flowers do not cope well with moisture. If you hang up fresh flowers to dry, the stems must not still be wet, and they shouldn't be wrapped in an impermeable material or hung in a damp room. Even when the drying process has removed all moisture from the flowers, they may grow moldy in rooms where there is high air moisture.

Care

Dried flowers are often considered to be dust magnets, but with regular care, the arrangements don't have to gather dust. Since moisture is bad for them, it's best to use a gentle blower or hairdryer to get rid of dust.

Handling

All dried flowers are much more fragile than when they are fresh. They become brittle and fragile during the drying phase. It's best, therefore, to be gentle with them, both when arranging them or otherwise handling them. And if something does break off or crumble, there's no need to panic. Small imperfections make them unique.

Materials

On the following pages, you'll find a list of flowers and seed heads that are well suited for dried flower arrangements. This list is by no means exhaustive but simply offers a first glimpse into the diverse world of dried flowers.

Flowers

Columbine—*Aquilegia*

Bishop's weed—*Ammi visnaga*

Dahlia—*Dahlia*

Sea holly—*Eryngium*

Edelweiss—*Leontopodium alpinium*

Flax—*Linum*

Lady's mantel—*Alchemilla*

Amaranth—*Amaranthus*

Rosehip—*Rosa*

Hydrangea—*Hydrangea*

Nigella—*Nigella*

Kangaroo paws—*Anigozanthos*

Globe amaranths—*Gomphrena*

Allium—*Allium*

Lavender—*Lavendula*

Mimosa—*Mimosa*

Poppy—*Papaver*

Daffodil—*Narcissus*

Peony—*Peonia*

Ranunculus—*Ranunculus*

Delphinium—*Delphinium*

Cattail—*Typha*

Rose—*Rosa*

Yarrow—*Achillea*

Baby's breath—*Gypsophila*

Scabiosa—*Scabiosa*

Sunflower—*Helianthus*

Masterwort—*Astrantia*

Sea lavender—*Limonium*

Straw flower / curry plant—*Helichrysum*

Billy buttons—*Craspedia*

Burnet—*Sanguisorba*

Bishop's lace—*Daucus carota*

Zinnia—*Zinnia*

Dahlia

Hydrangea

Lavender

Scabiosa

Helichrysum

Grasses

Silver Grass—*Miscanthus*

Barley—*Hordeum*

Phalaris—*Phalaris*

Bunnytail—*Lagurus*

Oat—*Avena*

Foxtail—*Setaria*

Pampas grass—*Cortaderia*

Reed—*Phragmites*

Wheat—*Triticum*

Quaking grass—*Briza*

Silver grass

Greenery and Branches

Box—*Buxus*

Eucalyptus—*Eucalyptus*

Fern—*Pteridophyte*

Ragwort—*Senecio*

Conifer—*Pinales*

Olive—*Olea*

Rosemary—*Rosmarinus*

Honesty—*Lunaria*

Asparagus—*Asparagus*

Thyme—*Thymus*

Pussy willow—*Salix*

Tools

To create wonderful arrangements from dried flowers, you'll need a few important utensils. You likely have many of them at home already; the others can be purchased at florists or craft stores.

- Natural raffia—It's used to tie down or tie together parts of the arrangement.

- Fleece wrapping tape—It's used to wrap around wreath blanks.

- Glue gun and glue sticks—They can be used in many ways to secure various materials; the glue is very hot when used, and the desired adhesive effect comes about as it cools.

- Wire cutters—They're the perfect tool for cutting winding wire, aluminum wire, or stub wires.

- Metal hoops in various colors, shaped hoops in various shapes, straw wreath blanks or floral foam bases (foam rings)

- Frog pin—It's used to secure floral foam on smooth surfaces, where there would otherwise not be any stable hold. It's attached using double-sided sticky tape or foam fix tack.

My Favorite Dried Flowers

I have put together an overview of my favorite dried flowers. I sometimes use the common names and sometimes the Latin names, depending on which names are commonly used by florists or in shops.

1. Sea lavender
2. Baby's breath
3. Lavender
4. Oat ears
5. Globe amaranths
6. Broom bloom
7. Ruscus
8. Hydrangea
9. Phalaris
10. Billy buttons
11. Bunnytail
12. Delphinium
13. Helichrysum
14. Poppy seed heads
15. Edelweiss
16. Flax
17. Kangaroo paws
18. Mimosa

19. Setaria

20. Thistles

21. Pampas grass

22. Roses

23. Honesty

24. Rhodanthe

25. Achillea (yarrow)

26. Glixia

27. Quaking grass

28. Ranunculus

29. Limonium

30. Eucalyptus

31. Ferns

32. Nigella

33. Ixodia

34. Pepperberries

35. Cape flowers

36. Wheat ears

Projects

Elegant in Gold

With the ever-increasing popularity of dried flowers, hoops in the form of partially decorated rings have become the go-to decor for the modern home. Be it natural or wild, playful or elegant, discrete or colorful, there's a perfect hoop for every taste and style.

Material

- Pampas grass
- Broom bloom
- Ixodia
- Ruscus

- Bunnytail, natural and pink
- Phalaris
- Metal hoop (12 in. in diameter), winding wire (0.01 in.), scissors

1. First, cut all the dried flowers to the correct length: pampas grass, broom bloom, and ixodia can be broken into individual stems. The individual leaves of the ruscus are cut off, and dried flowers with long stems, such as bunnytail and phalaris, are shortened accordingly (1).

2. You can either position the dried flowers on the hoop and tie in place with wire, or you can first make small bunches that you attach to the hoop (2a). The smaller the bunch, the easier it is to create the desired shape and design of the wreath. Ensure that newly positioned bunches of flowers completely cover the ends of the already attached dried flowers so that all the wire is hidden (2b).

3. Cover about half of the hoop with flowers. To create a clean finish with no visible wire, the final bunch is attached in the opposite direction to the other flowers. When doing so, ensure that you use more or less the same amount of the same materials as at the beginning to create a balanced appearance (3). You can cover the wire by gluing two to three dried flowerheads in position with a glue gun.

4. Once all the dried flowers are secured in the desired position, twist the wires on the back of the wreath and cut off any excess.

Flowers in Your Hair

A crown of dried flowers is a beautiful accessory for many occasions:
for weddings or bachelorette parties, for a celebration or a festival,
for birthday parties or christenings, or even for the first day at school.
If you keep the crown in a dry place and handle it with care, the delicate,
lightweight hair band will last for many years.

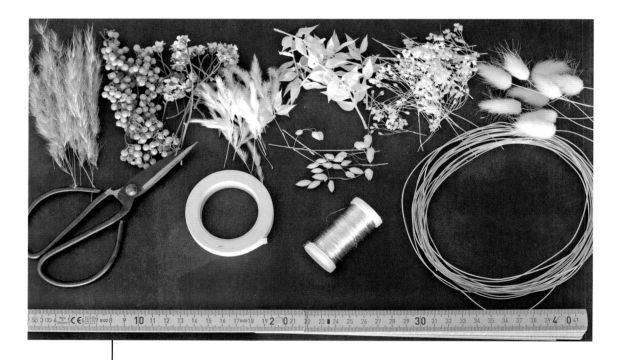

Materials

- Stabilized ruscus
- Broom bloom
- Bunnytail
- Ixodia
- Pampas grass
- Quaking grass

- Pepperberries, bleached
- Aluminum wire (0.04 in.),
  winding wire (0.01 in.), optional:
  jute wire, optional: coated
  winding wire, florist's tape, satin
  ribbon, scissors, measuring tape

1. Cut the aluminum wire to the required length, adding approximately 2–2.75 inches on each side. (For example, for a crown size of 16–16.5 inches, you'll need the wire to be 19.5–21 inches long). Make a small loop on both ends and twist in the rest of the wire (1).

2. For a better hold, wrap the aluminum wire with florist's tape (2). It prevents wires positioned next to each other from slipping. If you're using jute wire or coated wire, then this step isn't necessary.

3. Cut the dried flowers to length and prepare them for tying (3). Remove the leaves from the ends of the stems in order to attach the dried flowers more easily. Sharp edges should be removed or smoothed so that the crown will be more comfortable.

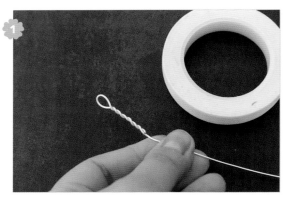

4. Position the individual stems or small bunches close to each other on the wire and secure with winding wire. The winding wire should be pulled as tightly as possible, while still ensuring that the stems, some of which are very delicate, don't snap (4).

5. Once you have fully decorated the aluminum wire from loop to loop, wrap the winding wire used to secure the flowers around the loop and thread it through on the wrong side.

6. To complete the crown, use a glue gun to stick the satin ribbon along the wrong side. It also protects the winding wire against slipping. There should be enough satin ribbon an either side to tie a bow at the back of the head (6a, 6b).

The great variety of dried flowers means there is absolutely no limit in terms of design and the color for your crown.

TIP

If the crown is open at the back and secured in place with the satin ribbon, then it allows for greater flexibility in terms of hair style. For this flexible style, the women's crown would be 16–16.5 in. long, while the girl's crown would be 14–14.5 in. long.

A Matter for the Heart

Small or big, for a special occasion or just because, out of love or regret,
fresh or dried—whenever flowers are given to a special person,
those flowers will certainly warm their heart.

Materials

- Dried roses with stems
- Stabilized hydrangea
- Globe amaranths
- Rhodanthe
- Mimosa
- Broom bloom

- Sea lavender
- Bunnytail
- Stabilized ruscus
- Heart-shaped bowl, floral foam, knife, scissors

1. First, cut the foam to fit the heart-shaped bowl, and place it in the bowl (1).

2. Start positioning the large-headed dried flowers in the foam. Distribute them evenly over the whole heart (2). This kind of flower generally has somewhat thicker stems. Although dried flowers don't need any water, their stalks are still cut diagonally with a knife when you are using foam, because the slanted cut gives the flowers a better hold in the foam. Now, add the small-headed dried flowers to completely fill any gaps. Working in this way will give you a beautiful, balanced harmonious appearance.

3. All the flowers in this heart decoration have more or less the same height. However, if a 3-D domed effect is desired, the dried flowers toward the center of the heart should become increasingly higher, while toward the edges of the heart, the flowers will have shorter stems. The 3-D shape is most effective when using a bowl with a large diameter.

TECHNIQUE: **"Flower Arranging with Foam"**
Green or black fresh-flower floral foam is recommended for use with dried flowers. This type of foam is very fine and soft, making it excellently suited to the delicate stems of dried flowers. However, unlike when used with fresh flowers, the foam is never wet when working with dried flowers. You should avoid pressing too hard into the foam; otherwise, the flowers won't find a hold.

If the inserted flower is not sitting perfectly, then it's best to find a new place to insert it instead of increasing the size of the hole by trying to reinsert it several times.

TIP
For a beautiful arrangement, the combination of plant materials is the most important aspect. You can use any kind of dried flowers that you have on hand. An arrangement appears particularly harmonious when there's a mixture of large-headed flowers (e.g., roses, hydrangea, globe amaranths, rhodanthe) and small-headed, delicate flowers (e.g., mimosa, broom bloom, sea lavender).

Eucalyptus Wreath

This wreath is created using different types of eucalyptus combined with other dried flowers. Eucalyptus is a very versatile foliage since it retains its wonderful scent for a long time and doesn't lose its shape after drying. When fresh, it's supple and easy to work with. There are no limits to the possible selection of the dried flowers. Skillfully put together, this wreath is a beautiful decoration for your wall or door.

Materials

- Different types of fresh eucalyptus (populus, cinerea, nicholii, parvifolia)
- Stabilized ruscus
- Broom bloom
- Setaria
- Bunnytail
- Sea lavender
- Grasses (e.g., pampas grass)

- Straw wreath blank (depending on the desired size of the finished wreath; a straw wreath with a diameter of 12 in. creates a finished wreath with an approximate diameter of 16 in.)
- Green fleece wrapping tape, mossing pins, winding wire (0.01 in.), scissors, secateurs

1. Prepare by cutting the eucalyptus and the dried flowers to the desired lengths. The longer the stalks, the bushier the wreath will be.

2. Wrap the straw wreath with the fleece tape so it's completely covered, and secure the ends with mossing pins. The tape prevents the light-colored straw from showing through on the finished wreath (2a, 2b).

3. Wrap the winding wire once around the wreath and twist the ends so that the wire stays in place while working with the flowers. To secure it, wrap the wire a few more times around the wreath and pull it tight (3).

4. If you're right-handed, you'll add the flowers in a clockwise direction. That means you place the material on the wreath from left to right (the tips point to the left and the stalk ends to the right). If you're left-handed, you'll work in the opposite direction.

5. Row by row, tie the different types of eucalyptus and dried flowers in place. For each row, use your left hand to hold a sufficient amount of dried flowers in position, then use your right hand to wrap the wire one or two times over the stems and pull tight. The next row is positioned very close to the previous row, so that all the stems from the previous row are covered and there are no gaps (5).

6. To finish, push the stalks of the last row of dried flowers under the first row and carefully secure them by wrapping the wire several times around them (6). Ensure that there are no gaps between the final row and the first row of dried flowers and that the transition is barely visible. If there are gaps in the wreath, they can subsequently be filled with more flowers that are secured with pins.

7. Cut the winding wire and thread it under the wire on the back of the wreath, wrap it around the wire on the back several times, and insert the ends into the straw wreath.

Ostrich Egg Vase

If you're looking for some special Easter decorations, you can create a surefire highlight with an ostrich egg decorated with dried flowers.

Materials

- Ostrich egg
- Stabilized ruscus
- Broom bloom
- Oat ears
- Bunnytail
- Phalaris
- Rhodanthe, pink
- Pampas grass
- Feathers
- Floral foam, spray paint (in desired color), wire cutter / pliers, frog pin, scissors

1. First, make a large opening in the ostrich egg. An ostrich egg is very robust; compared to a hen or goose egg, it's very hard to break. Therefore, effort and intuition are required to increase the size of the hole already present in the egg. It's possible to cut in a hole, however; such a hole would be very neat. A natural-looking hole can be made by carefully breaking away the shell with wire cutters or pliers (1).

2. Once you've created the desired opening, spray the egg with black spray paint. So that no undesired fingerprints get on the egg, balance the egg on a stick or cane to paint and dry it (2a, 2b).

3. Cut floral foam to fit in the egg up to the height of the opening (3). For better hold, you can secure the foam to the bottom of the egg, using double-sided sticky tape and a frog pin (the green plastic item on the picture of the materials).

4. Cut the dried flowers to the desired height and carefully insert them into the foam. They can be rather short so that the heads just protrude slightly over the top of the egg. However, if you want a more playful look, leave the stems longer and arrange the flowers more loosely. Finally, you can add a few delicate feathers to the ostrich egg as decoration.

5. Place the finished ostrich egg on a nest of twigs or feathers so that it doesn't roll over (5).

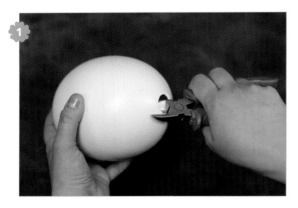

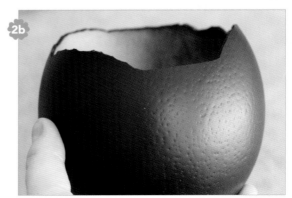

TIP

If you want to save yourself the effort of enlarging the hole, you can make do with the small hole that the egg already has. After spraying and drying the egg, you can simply place a few flowers or stems of grass in this hole. An ostrich egg in this fashion is also very decorative and adds interest to your Easter décor.

An Easter Hoop

Dried flower arrangements can wonderfully reflect seasons or holidays. The spring is shown in delicate and light flowers, while the summer is full of color. Autumn expresses itself in earthy shades, and winter is a snow-white dream. With the right colors and materials, any dried arrangement can be the perfect accompaniment to the season.

Materials

- Fresh box
- Stabilized ruscus
- Phalaris
- Pampas grass
- Stabilized fern

- Blown quail eggs
- Feathers
- Metal hoop (12 in. diameter), jute cord, winding wire (0.01 in.), different types of ribbons, scissors, hot-glue gun

1. Wrap a jute cord around the metal hoop so that the hoop is half covered. To get a better hold, you can secure the cord by using a glue gun. Apply the hot glue to a few places on the metal hoop and tightly wrap the cord around it (1).

2. Place two to three stems of box on the half of the hoop not covered in cord, then wrap the wire around them several times and pull tight. Then, add more dried flowers and secure them with the winding wire (2).

3. In this way, attach all the dried flowers until you reach the other end of the cord on the hoop. Cut the stems of the last bunch short and wrap the end of the cord over them and secure with the glue gun so that there is a neat join (3).

4. Use the glue gun to stick the quail eggs and the feathers to the finished wreath.

5. Attach more feathers to a separate piece of wire, ensuring the gaps between them are even (5). Add this decorative feathered wire with other pieces of ribbon and jute cord to the wreath as additional decoration.

TIP

After Easter, the quail eggs can be removed, and the hoop can be used the whole year through.

With Love for Mommy

There's more to beautiful dried-flower hoops than just tying flowers
to the hoop itself; dried flowers within the hoop are also very decorative.
Let me present a different take on a dried flower wreath.

Materials

- Bunnytail
- Phalaris
- Stabilized ruscus
- Broom bloom
- Helichrysum
- Thistle
- Ixodia

- Pampas grass
- Metal hoop (at least 16 in. in diameter), aluminum wire (0.04 in.), winding wire, florist's tape, scissors, wire cutters, cloth ribbons of various widths and materials

How To

1. To create a pretty shape for the letters, we will use a 0.04 in. thick aluminum wire. It's very supple, yet it stays in shape after bending it. This means that the finished lettering can be easily attached to the hoop later. Depending on the hoop and ring size, at least 3.5-4 ft. of wire is required.

2. To prevent the flowers from slipping on the smooth surface of the wire, you should first wrap the wire with florist tape. When you're winding the tape, you should stretch it, and it will yield—a little like crepe paper. The stretching releases the adhesive so that the florist tape will stick to it well (2).

3. Slowly bend the wrapped wire into the shape of the required letters, ensuring the letters are joined to each other (3).

4. Shorten the dried flower stems and prepare them to be tied to the letters. The smaller or narrower the writing should be, the more delicately you'll need to work so that the letters do not appear to merge into each other (4).

5. Position the dried flowers stem by stem on the wire and secure with the winding wire. Pull the wire tight after every wrap; however, be aware the some of the flowers have very delicate stems that break easily. You can carefully move the aluminum wire to make this process easier. After the flowers are attached, you just need to reshape the letters.

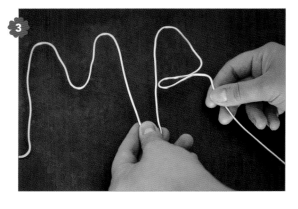

6. To attach the lettering to the metal hoop, spread hot glue on the outer edge of the first and last letters and then quickly press them into the hoop. The adhesive effect should occur instantly.

7. Finally, attach a selection of ribbons to the bottom of the hoop, using lark's-head knots. And voilà, a hoop for Mothers' Day, for a birthday, or to celebrate a birth has been created with much thought and love.

Dried Flower Bouquet

A bouquet made of dried flowers has been and remains a true classic with endless variations, using different materials. When arranging them, you must remember that in the drying process, the stems of the dried flowers have lost their elasticity and are therefore not as flexible as fresh flowers. They can easily be bent or even snapped, which is why care is needed when arranging them.

Materials

- Pampas grass
- Dried hydrangea
- Reed
- Dried or fresh eucalyptus
- Bunnytail
- Craspedia
- Wheat ears
- Poppy head
- Stabilized ruscus
- Sea lavender
- Baby's breath
- Stabilized fern
- Natural raffia, stub wire, florist tape, secateurs, wire cutters

🔴 TECHNIQUE: **"Cutting To Size"**

Certain materials, such as pampas grass or hydrangea heads, are generally too long (the pampas grass can measure 32–40 in. long) or too bushy (it's not rare for a hydrangea head to have a diameter of 8 in. or more) to be inserted into a bouquet in one piece. Therefore, they are cut up to make smaller stems (1). If some parts of the plant have only very short stems (2), you can still use them in a bouquet if the stem is attached to a stub wire. For a tall stem, a thick stub wire (approximately 0.03 in.) is inserted into the end of the stem. For flowers with a closed stem, the stub wire is placed next to the stem and secured with florist tape (3 and 4). Once you have created these false wire stems, they can be added to a bouquet (5 and 6).

1. Prepare all the dried flowers you've select-

ed for the bouquet. A mixture of flowers and grasses with different densities, head sizes, and structures create a particularly beautiful look. Remove any superfluous leaves from the stems and, if required, attach to stud wires or cut them smaller. Select a main stem (in this case, a pampas grass frond) around which the other dried flowers will be positioned. Add the dried flowers stem by stem, always working in the same direction. Hold the flowers tightly in place with your thumb, index finger, and middle finger (1).

2. When tying the flowers, if you notice a gap or several of the same flowers together, you can also add or remove flowers from above (2). To do so, loosen your grip, and when the added stalk is in place, you can tighten it again. Around the sides, the bouquet should open out more, so position the dried flowers more horizontally and with shorter stems.

3. When all the flowers are in place and you're happy with the bouquet, tie the stems together with natural raffia. Wrap it around several times and secure in place with a knot (3).

Photo Wreath

Hanging photos in picture frames is the traditional way to display them.
However, the current trend is for innovative new ways to display photos.
One example is a photo wreath—it's bound to become an eye-catcher
on your wall, and this pretty idea is very easy to make.
And the best thing about it: you can quickly and easily
swap in recent photos.

Materials

- Fresh eucalyptus
- Stabilized ruscus
- Pampas grass
- Bunnytail
- Phalaris
- Dried ranunculus
- Ferns
- Honesty
- Wood hoop (28 in. diameter), cotton ribbon, stapler, jute cord, paper and bulldog clips, scissors, photos

How To

1. Cut the wide cotton ribbon into lengths and stretch them over the hoop. Secure in place on the back of the hoop with a stapler (1a and 1b).

2. To make the floral decoration for the wreath a little denser, make small bunches of flowers and attach them to the hoop (2).

3. It's a good idea to make the small bunches before you start attaching them to the hoop. Tie the bunches together with winding wire. Doing this preparation means you can attach the flowers more quickly.

4. Attaching the bunches of dried flowers is not significantly different from attaching individual stems. The little bunches overlap on the ring so that the stalks of the previous bunches are covered. Once it's in a suitable position, wrap the bunch several times with the wire and pull it tight. Keep repeating this process until the hoop has the desired shape and density. The bigger the bunches, the denser the wreath. To give it a balanced appearance, you can add individual stems at the end.

5. To give the photo hanger a pretty appearance, wrap jute cord around a few centimeters of the final, visible stalks. Knot the cord on the back of the hoop or secure it with a glue gun. Optionally, you can also wrap the whole hoop with the cord (5). It adds a pretty accent of color that could reflect the colors of the dried flowers used.

Spruced Up with Dried Flowers

You can use dried flowers

to add beautiful accents in many ways.

Table Decorations

For instance, a few arranged dried flowers can add a highlight to your table for Sunday brunch. They add color and a special flair.

Make small bunches from a selection of dried flowers and wrap them with wire. They look prettiest when the flowers are arranged at different heights: pampas grass or feather grass for airiness right at the top, bunnytail or phalaris filling out the middle, and finally two delicate flowers at the bottom of the bunch. Place this bunch on a serviette and secure with a piece of jute cord.

Gift Wrapping with Great Effect

A small bunch of flowers tied in the same way is also perfect for decorating a gift box. The little bunch can be attached with a small piece of double-sided sticky tape or a thin strip of hot glue from the glue gun. So prettily decorated, even a small present gives the recipient a lot of joy.

But an expensive gift can become even more attractive with dried-flower adornments; for example, a voucher packed in natural paper. Use a broad strip of dark paper as a contrast background for the dried flowers. Attach this

strip to the gift with a piece of double-sided sticky tape. Stick a slightly narrower piece of see-through ribbon onto it. Now you can insert the dried flowers under or through the ribbon, creating a 3-D effect. If required, you can add more cord or ribbon horizontally to provide a better hold. And voilà, a gift full of love.

Floral Greeting Card

Luckily, the custom of sending cards has not yet gone completely out of fashion in our digital age. Be it birthday or get-well-soon cards, to say congratulations or simply thank you, it can all be expressed with a pretty card. And what could possibly be more beautiful than a stylish handmade card? It clearly articulates that your greeting is heartfelt.

You can buy blank cards with envelopes in any well-stocked stationers. There is no limit when creating the cards. However, it's worth selecting flatter dried flowers and then pressing them overnight under a few heavy books. Use florist's glue or superglue to affix the flowers on the cards, and, for additional hold, cover the stalk ends with a lace ribbon. Add a sticker or a sweet message, and you've made a very personal greeting card.

Floral Gift Tags

Even a handmade gift tag can be enhanced with dried flowers. You can make the tag with air-drying modeling clay. Roll it out so that it is approximately 0.2 in. thick. You can use a small clean bottle to do this. Use a round object (e.g., a small bowl or glass) as the cutter. Use a blade for straight edges.

Once you've created the desired shape, you can use a stamp to imprint a message or image on it, with or without color. Mini bunches of flowers are pressed into the tag and secured with a strip of clay. Use a wooden stick to make a hole for hanging. After 24 hours, the clay will be dry, and you can use the tag.

One Wreath Four Ways

A beautiful dried flower wreath can almost always be used in several ways.
Thanks to the long life of the flowers, the wreath can be presented
in new ways throughout the year.

Materials

- Pampas grass
- Fresh eucalyptus
- Stabilized ruscus
- Bunnytail
- Quaking grass
- Stabilized fern
- Ixodia
- Rhodanthe, white
- Baby's breath
- Floral foam ring (10 in. diameter), scissors, knife

Hung Up

Will the dried flowers to decorate a wall?

Of course, and they are always beautiful.

1. When selecting the material, make sure you choose a balanced mixture of different sizes and textures. Pampas grass, eucalyptus, ruscus, flower heads, bunnytail, quaking grass, and fern are all well suited. They are all different, but they all come wonderfully together to create a harmonious arrangement with a lot of charm.

2. Cut all materials to the required length (see Technique: "Cutting to Size," p. 86). Cut firmer stalks, such as eucalyptus, diagonally so that they will have a better hold in the foam (2). Stalks that are squashed, bent, or split while making the wreath can be cut again and reinserted.

3. To help you find the correct mixture of dried flowers, insert some of the desired materials into a small area of the foam ring as a test. If the result is convincing, then you can continue working on the whole wreath (3).

4. Ensure that the flowers and grasses on the inside of the wreath are shorter so that the center is not covered, allowing, for example, a pretty storm lamp to be inserted into it.

Now, the finished wreath just needs to find a purpose.

TIP

A wreath made using floral foam appears similar to one with a straw wreath base; however, it's more robust and bushier. The base is always a few centimeters thicker than a metal hoop, meaning that the wreath automatically has more volume. Compared to tying the material to a hoop, using foam allows the material to be worked in several directions, which creates movement and a certain lightness.

Hurricane Lamp

When the weather is getting nicer and the porch
needs a new decoration, simply place a hurricane lamp
in the center of the wreath. It looks so inviting.

ⓘ TECHNIQUE: "Cutting to Size"

Frequently, an arrangement doesn't require a whole long stem, which may also have individual sprays growing on it. To make the best possible use of the material, it's a good idea to cut the stems to suit your needs.

For instance, you can cut off individual sprays from the main stem of ruscus and remove the lower leaves on each branch, since they would only get in the way when the smaller stems are inserted into floral foam or tied into a bunch (1).

For baby's breath, which has many sprays, you should cut off the smaller sprays as required (2). You can also deploy the same technique for flower heads, such as ixodia or rhodanthe. They often grow flowers in groups that have to be separated when arranging (3).

The same applies to grasses of all kinds. One frond with many small stems provides a significant amount of material (4).

Even fern is no exception. The delicate leaves of a stabilized fern can be used individually with a wonderful effect (5).

Eucalyptus and other fresh greenery, such as olive branches or box, produce a lot of material when the branches are taken apart. When cutting, it's important to always keep a piece of stem that you'll be able to insert into the foam (6).

A Great Idea

Your guests are coming, but the table looks empty. Simply add a pretty bowl filled with the dried flower wreath and ta-da!

Hurricane Lamp

Dried flowers can be used for many diverse purposes, and they turn day-to-day objects into enchanting highlights. With the creative application of dried flowers, a simple jar becomes a beautiful summer decoration for the porch.

Materials

- Bunnytail
- Phalaris
- Fern
- Broom bloom
- Stabilized lunaria
- Pampas grass
- Jar, two rubber bands, candle, colored pellets, cloth ribbon or cord, scissors, glue gun

1. Place the two rubber bands around the jar. They should have a firm hold and not be too loose. You'll use them to hold the dried flowers in position and prevent them from slipping (1).

2. Insert the stems under the two elastic bands, arranging the flowers so that they go all the way round the jar.

3. To create a harmonious effect, use stems of different lengths. It also ensures that there are no gaps on the jar. Be careful that none of the flammable dried flowers hang over the edge of the jar (3).

TIP

If the jar is to be repurposed, the remains of the glue gun can be removed without leaving any residue.

4. Once you have positioned all the dried flowers as desired, secure the ends of the stalks with a glue gun. Take a wide cloth ribbon and apply glue bit by bit to the jar or the ribbon. Firmly press the ribbon over the ends of the stems (4). The hot glue adheres within a few seconds, so you can immediately move on to the next step.

   WARNING: The glue that comes out of the glue gun is very hot. Ensure that you take extra care when handling the glue gun so as not to get burned.

5. Tie another ribbon around the center of the jar so that the dried flowers are given extra hold (5a). As soon as you have tied this ribbon firmly in place, you can carefully remove the rubber bands (5b).

6. Add decorative pellets of your choice to the jar. The pellets mean that the candle will have a stable hold. Many jars have a curved base, and the pellets even it out (6).

Sweet Ice Cream

An ice cream cone, a small piece of floral foam,
dried flowers of your choice, and ta-da!—you have a unique gift,
perfect as a hostess gift for a cool summer or birthday party.

Fill the upper part of the cone with a piece of foam
so that the dried flowers have a good hold and won't easily fall out.
The incredible diversity of dried flowers
ensures a colorful decoration.

It's guaranteed to make the recipients, especially children, smile.

Dried Flower Arrangement

Not only are dried flower arrangements a nice way
to decorate your own four walls, but they're also gaining importance
in the field of commerce. For instance, elegant dried flowers decorate tables
in the gastronomy industry, or larger arrangements grace the reception
desks of offices, hotels, and medical practices,
replacing faded artificial flowers.

Materials

- Different types of eucalyptus
- Olive branches
- Pampas grass and other grasses
- Dried palm leaves
- Wheat ears
- Bunnytail
- Setaria
- Fern
- Sea lavender
- Plant pot, chicken wire (either zinc coated or painted green), wire cutters, scissors

(!) TECHNIQUE: "Using Chicken Wire for Arrangements"

Florists frequently use chicken wire when working with fresh flowers, and it's very suitable for dried flower arrangements too. You'll need chicken wire with small holes in order to form a frame in the vase or plant pot that will give the flowers a good hold. A great advantage of this technique is that you can change the position of the flower stems as often as you desire.

Squash down the chicken wire so that it fits into the vase or plant pot (1). It's important that when squashing the chicken wire, you create several levels, which will support the flowers in several places (2).

TIP

When inserting flowers and grasses, either in chicken wire or foam, the center of the arrangement should always be the highest point. The arrangement should flatten out toward the edges. That means that you always use shorter stems on the sides to achieve a slightly rounded dome shape.

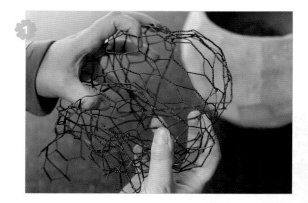

1. Prepare the vase or plant pot by adding chicken wire as described.

2. Cut the dried flowers so that they have longer stems. In this way, the arrangement gains a nice volume.

3. Start inserting the branches of eucalyptus and olive. They form a basic framework to which you can add the other dried flowers (3).

4. Then add the grasses and palm leaves, which give the arrangement the necessary density. Proceed to add material with thin stalks such as wheat ears, setaria, and bunnytail—such additions generate more movement. Finally, fill the gaps with sea lavender and ferns, which create a loose effect.

When working on an arrangement, it's a good idea to hold the stems of the dried flowers in the required position, in order to establish how long they should be cut. Only once it has been cut should you put the stem in its final position.

A Diamond-Shaped Wreath

Hydrangeas can be used in their fresh, dried, or stabilized forms. However, depending on their state, they have different characteristics that should be considered when using them.

Materials

- Dried or stabilized hydrangeas
- Bunnytail
- Phalaris
- Baby's breath
- Stabilized ruscus
- Pampas grass
- Diamond-shaped metal hoop, winding wire, scissors

Hydrangeas are one of the most popular plants in our gardens. Therefore, they're perfect to be integrated in dried flower arrangements. Fresh hydrangeas are suitable only once they have passed their peak, and their resplendent colors start to fade (1, 2).

At this stage, cut hydrangeas will not wilt without water but instead start to dry. With low exposure to sunlight, they can be kept for years. However, dried hydrangeas are difficult to work with because their delicate stems can be easily snapped. As the saying goes, they should be handled with kid gloves.

In contrast, stabilized hydrangeas have undergone a chemical process so that they are very supple and flexible. It also makes them easy to use. However, they're also very delicate, and their almost transparent flowers can be easily accidentally ripped off.

1. Attaching the dried flowers to the diamond is like tying them to a hoop. However, two different sections of the metal diamond are decorated (1).

2. Dried flowers with short stems are well suited to this project. They are tied into small bunches and wrapped with wire (2). To create a clean finish, the final flowers in both sections are attached in opposite directions (see p. 48).

3. Use two to three dried flower heads to cover where the final bunch is attached. Secure them with a glue gun (3).

TIP: The diamond shape is excellently suited for "double-sided tying." Dried flower wreathes and hoops generally have a front side, which is decorated, and a backside, where the attachment process is visible. That is not a problem when they are hung on a wall or door, or when placed on a table or tray. However, when the wreath is hung at a window or hangs in the center of a room so that both sides are visible, the backside will appear unsightly. To avoid this, when making the wreath, position the dried flowers both on the front side and backside and secure them with wire. However, this process is somewhat more difficult because you have to keep an eye on both sides as you work.

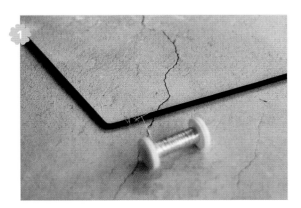

Double Hoop

The binding technique for this wreath is not greatly different from the previously described techniques. However, what makes it special is the combination of two partially decorated wreaths and how they are arranged together.

Materials

- Bunnytail
- Phalaris
- Baby's breath
- Stabilized hydrangea
- Stabilized ruscus
- Broom bloom

- Stabilized or fresh eucalyptus
- 2 metal hoops in different sizes (e.g., 8 in. and 16 in. diameter), scissors, woolen cord, wooden sign, winding wire

1. First, decorate both hoops (see p. 128). The area decorated with dried flowers should be the same proportion on each hoop. It's a good idea to work the largest hoop first and then use it as a guide.

2. Now both hoops can be joined together. To do so, lay both rings on a flat surface. Secure them together with winding wire and then wrap woolen cord around the wire (2).

3. The double hoop can also be separated again, or the two hoops could be simply hung next to each other or even together with a third hoop. They make a good composition and are very well suited for bare, neutral walls.

4. Hoops with lettering saying "Home" or "Welcome" or with names or sweet messages ("Best Mom" or "My Sweetheart") are very trendy. Corresponding wood lettering can be easily integrated in an already finished wreath. In this way, the larger wreath can be enhanced and fulfill a new decorative purpose (4).

Flowers in Glass

Placing dried flowers in glass is a very beautiful,
decorative idea. These arrangements are very well suited as gifts.
Just a few flowers can create a great effect.

Materials

- Leftover dried flowers
- Clear glass container, floral foam / frog pin, tweezers, LED light string and cork set, ribbons, cords, pendants, candle

If dried flowers got broken when working on other projects or if you accidentally cut too many flower stems too short, so that they cannot be used, then they can be put to one side for a pretty glass décor project.

A glass bottle without a bottom and with a re-movable wooden stopper is very well suited for this type of arrangement. The bottles are decorated with your choice of dried flowers, which you insert into floral foam. A combination of large flower heads with more-delicate stems gives a harmonious result. The foam helps you precisely and safely position the dried flowers as you desire. To add even more atmosphere, you can add a cork with fairy lights (1).

Use tweezers to place the dried flowers into glass vessels with a bottom and a narrow neck. First, position the flowers at the bottom of the bottle and then add flowers with longer stems right up to the top of the bottle. Just a few stems create a great effect. The vessel can be sealed with a lid or a cork. Depending on the neck size, the bottle can also be used as a candleholder for tapered candles.

A very popular decorative variation is dried flowers under a glass bell jar. You can use a frog pin instead of foam. The frog pin can be secured to the bottom of the bell jar with dou-ble-sided sticky tape and decorated with dried flowers. It is not necessary to cut the thicker stems diagonally. The biggest advantage of frog pins over floral foam is that they can be used again.

Concrete Heart

When people talk about dried flowers, they often think of
a few stems in a chic vase, a bouquet, or a stylish hoop. However,
dried flowers can be used for very different objects of art that enrich the
home. There's no limit to the artistic use of them. One example is
creating concrete art. Concrete art can be tailored to its location
and your personal preferences in terms of color and material.

Dried Flower Materials

- Stabilized ruscus
- Bunnytail
- Ixodia
- Sea lavender
- Baby's breath
- Stabilized poppy
- Pampas grass
- Scissors

Material for Pouring Concrete

- Cement
- Quartz sand
- Water
- Picture frame with raised edges
- Paper/card

- Polystyrene
- Masking tape
- Pen, sharp knife, bowl, stick for mixing, small brush

It's a good idea to prepare all the materials, including the dried flowers, in advance so that everything is ready and you can start decorating immediately after the concrete has been poured.

1. First, prepare the picture frame (without glass). Use a double layer of masking tape to cover any gaps on the back of the frame (1a). Cover the front with masking tape to keep from making a mess when pouring the concrete and to get a neat edge when removing it from the frame (1b).

2. Transfer the heart template, which has been cut from a piece of paper or card, to the polystyrene (2a). Use a sharp knife to cut the heart out of the polystyrene so that the empty heart shape remains (2b).

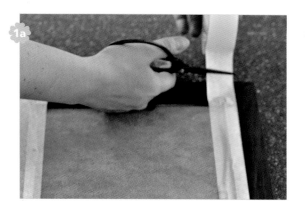

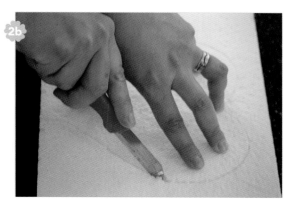

3. Now it's time to mix the concrete. According to the amount required for the size of the frame, mix one part cement with one part quartz sand in a bowl. Mix well and add water until it is a homogenous moist mass (3a). Pour the concrete up to the masking tape in the picture frame and smooth over (3b). Gently shake so that air bubbles are eliminated and the surface becomes smooth.

4. In the final step, the polystyrene heart cutout is secured to the picture frame so that it doesn't slip as you add the dried flowers (4).

1. Start inserting the flowers immediately after the concrete has been poured. Ensure that the stalks have a good hold and are inserted as far as possible into the concrete. Add the flowers one by one evenly over the whole surface (1). The stalks should be inserted next to each other rather than several stems being inserted into the same place. In this way, the delicate stems do not fall out once the concrete has hardened.

2. When the heart is fully decorated with dried flowers, remove the polystyrene carefully so that there are no marks in the concrete (2a). Before putting the picture somewhere safe to dry for 24 to 36 hours, check that all the flowers are secure. Remove the masking tape (2b).

3. After drying, use a fine brush to remove the powdery layer from the surface of the concrete, and now you have a durable artwork for your home.

Other Schiffer Books on
Related Subjects:

Forever Flowers: Dry, Preserve, Display, Antonia De Vere,
ISBN 978-0-7643-6207-1
Endless Florescence: Transformative Contemporary Dried Floral Design,
Jenny Thomasson, ISBN 978-0-7643-6430-3
Wreaths: Fresh, Foliage, Foraged, and Faux, Alys Dobbie,
 ISBN 978-0-7643-6212-5

Originally published as *Trockenblumen & Floral Hoops* © 2021 Christophorus Verlag / Christian Verlag GmbH, Munich. Translated from the German by Catherine Venner.

Library of Congress Control Number: 2023931153

Cover design by Ashley Millhouse
Photos and styling: Ivana Jost
Type set in Andes

ISBN: 978-0-7643-6689-5
Printed in China

Published by Schiffer Publishing, Ltd.
4880 Lower Valley Road
Atglen, PA 19310
Phone: (610) 593-1777; Fax: (610) 593-2002
Email: Info@schifferbooks.com
Web: www.schifferbooks.com

For our complete selection of fine books on this and related subjects, please visit our website at www.schifferbooks.com. You may also write for a free catalog.

Schiffer Publishing's titles are available at special discounts for bulk purchases for sales promotions or premiums. Special editions, including personalized covers, corporate imprints, and excerpts, can be created in large quantities for special needs. For more information, contact the publisher.

We are always looking for people to write books on new and related subjects. If you have an idea for a book, please contact us at proposals@schifferbooks.com.

FSC
www.fsc.org
MIX
Paper | Supporting responsible forestry
FSC® C104723

About the Author

IVANA JOST has always been strongly attracted by the beauty of nature and mountains. As an independent event and wedding florist, she has been able to fully live out this passion for nature and its materials since 2018 by successfully running her company, Das Blumenatelier. She lives in Upper Bavaria, Germany, with her husband and two children.